Plus

Bugs, Bugs, Bugs!

Wasps

by Margaret Hall

Consulting Editor: Gail Saunders-Smith, PhD

Consultant: Laura Jesse, Extension Associate
Department of Entomology
Iowa State University
Ames, Iowa

Capstone
press

Mankato, Minnesota

Pebble Plus is published by Capstone Press,
151 Good Counsel Drive, P.O. Box 669, Mankato, Minnesota 56002.
www.capstonepress.com

1 2 3 4 5 6 10 09 08 07 06 05

Library of Congress Cataloging-in-Publication Data
Hall, Margaret, 1947–
 Wasps / by Margaret Hall.
     p. cm.—(Pebble Plus. Bugs, bugs, bugs!)
 Includes bibliographical references and index.
 ISBN 0-7368-4254-3 (hardcover)
 1. Wasps—Juvenile literature. I. Title.
 QL565.2.H34 2006
 595.79'8—dc22   2004029488
Summary: Simple text and photographs describe the physical characteristics of wasps.

Editorial Credits
Heather Adamson, editor; Linda Clavel, set designer; Ted Williams, book designer; Jo Miller, photo researcher;
 Scott Thoms, photo editor

Photo Credits
Brand X Pictures, back cover
Corbis/Neil Miller; Papillio, 11
James P. Rowan, front cover
KAC Productions/Rolf Nussbaumer, 6–7
Nature Picture Library/Premaphotos, 18–19
Pete Carmichael, 13
Photo Researchers, Inc./Stephen Dalton, 9; Gary Meszaros, 14–15; Kenneth H. Thomas, 17; Scott Camazine, 21
Photri Microstock, 1
SuperStock, 5

Note to Parents and Teachers

The Bugs, Bugs, Bugs! set supports national science standards related to divesity of life
and heredity. This book describes and illustrates wasps. The images support early readers
in understanding the text. The repetition of words and phrases helps early readers learn
new words. This book also introduces early readers to subject-specific vocabulary words,
which are defined in the Glossary section. Early readers may need assistance to read
some words and to use the Table of Contents, Glossary, Read More, Internet Sites, and
Index sections of the book.

Table of Contents

What Are Wasps?

Wasps are flying insects.

They move

their wings quickly.

5

How Wasps Look

Most wasps have yellow,
black, or dark blue bodies.

Most wasps are
about the size
of a paper clip.

Wasps have two antennas.

They smell and feel

with their antennas.

antennas

Most female wasps
have sharp stingers.
Male wasps
do not have stingers.

stinger

What Wasps Do

Wasps sometimes use
their stingers to kill insects
for food.
Most wasps eat nectar
from flowers.

Some wasps make paper
by chewing wood. Wasps use
the paper to build nests.
Many wasps live in each nest.

Some wasps build small nests
out of mud.
They live alone.

Wasps lay eggs
in their nests.
Young wasps hatch
and grow in the nests.

21

Glossary

antenna—a feeler; insects use antennas to sense movement, to smell, and to listen to each other.

female—an animal that can give birth to young animals or lay eggs

insect—a small animal with a hard outer shell, six legs, three body sections, and two antennas; most insects have wings.

male—an animal that can father young

stinger—a sharp part that sticks out of the back end of some insects' bodies

Read More

Frost, Helen. *Wasps.* Insects. Mankato, Minn.: Pebble Books, 2001.

Miller, Sara Swan. *Ants, Bees, and Wasps of North America.* Animals in Order. New York: Franklin Watts, 2003.

Townsend, John. *Incredible Insects.* Raintree Freestyle. Chicago: Raintree, 2005.

Internet Sites

FactHound offers a safe, fun way to find Internet sites related to this book. All of the sites on FactHound have been researched by our staff.

Here's how:

1. Visit *www.facthound.com*

2. Type in this special code **0736842543** for age-appropriate sites. Or enter a search word related to this book for a more general search.

3. Click on the **Fetch It** button.

FactHound will fetch the best sites for you!

Index

Word Count: 112
Grade: 1
Early-Intervention Level: 13